UNIFORMITY
with
GOD'S WILL

FROM THE ITALIAN
OF
ST. ALPHONSUS DE LIGUORI

By
THOMAS W. TOBIN, C.SS.R.

TAN Books
Charlotte, North Carolina

Imprimi Potest: John J. Sephton, C.SS.R.
                 Provincial
                 Nov. 21, 1951

Nihil Obstat: John J. Walsh, S.J.
                 Diocesan Censor

Imprimatur: Richard J. Cushing
                 Archbishop of Boston
                 January 5, 1952

ISBN: 978-0-89555-019-4

Printed and bound in the United States of America

TAN Books
Charlotte, North Carolina
2010

PREFACE

In Volume 1, *Opere Ascetiche di S. Alfonso M. de Liguori,* Roma, 1933, "Uniformity with God's Will" is included as one of three works under the heading, "Lesser Works on Divine Love." There is no preface in the Italian original. However, it has been thought well to provide one here.

Prof. Candido M. Romano[1] says this brochure was written probably in 1755, as appears from a letter by the Saint, under date of Nov. 2, 1755, to Sister Giannastasio, at Cava. Romano goes on to say:

> "This (i.e. God's will) was for Alphonsus a theme of predilection, a theme dearest to his heart. Just as St. Ignatius stressed 'the greater glory of God,' St. Alphonsus in all his works, gave prominence to 'the greater good pleasure of God.' Most likely the occasion that brought forth this treatise was the death, in 1753, of Father Paul Cafaro, C.SS.R., St. Alphonsus' confessor and director. The death of this worthy priest deeply affected the Saint and he expressed his sentiments in a poem on God's will. The wide acclaim it received may have suggested to him the thought that a tract on the same subject would be helpful to the souls of others. If this be true, his surmise proved correct, for the appearance of his subsequent pamphlet was greeted with instant favor."

Cardinal Villecourt, in his *Life of St. Alphonsus,* quotes long passages from this pamphlet and ends by saying: "Our Saint frequently read it himself and when his sight had failed he arranged to have it read to him by others."

This brochure bears the stamp of Alphonsian simplicity of style and solidity of doctrine. Moreover the instances he cites from the lives of the saints have a gentle graciousness and contain a fragrance that is redolent of the Fioretti of St. Francis of Assisi.

Through God's grace and our Lady's prayers may a diligent reading of the book bring us far along the way of perfection by the cultivation of uniformity with God's holy will!

Thomas W. Tobin, C.Ss.R.

Oct. 16, 1951
Feast of St. Gerard Majella, C.Ss.R.

UNIFORMITY WITH GOD'S WILL

1.
Excellence of This Virtue

Perfection is founded entirely on the love of God: "Charity is the bond of perfection" (*Col.* 3:14); and perfect love of God means the complete union of our will with God's: "The principal effect of love is so to unite the wills of those who love each other as to make them will the same things."[1] It follows then, that the more one unites his will with the divine will, the greater will be his love of God. Mortification, meditation, receiving Holy Communion, acts of fraternal charity are all certainly pleasing to God—but only when they are in accordance with his will. When they do not accord with God's will, he not only finds no pleasure in them, but he even rejects them utterly and punishes them.

To illustrate: A man has two servants. One works unremittingly all day long, but according to his own devices; the other, conceivably, works less, but he does do what he is told. This latter of course is going to find favor in the eyes of his master; the other will not. Now, in applying this example, we may ask: Why should we perform actions for God's glory if they are not going to be acceptable to him? God does not want sacrifices, the prophet Samuel told King Saul, but he does want obedience to his will: "Doth the Lord desire holocausts and victims, and not rather that the voice of the Lord should be obeyed? For obedience is better than sacrifices; and to hearken rather than to offer the fat of rams. Because it is like the sin of witchcraft to rebel; and like the crime of idolatry to refuse to obey" (*1 Kgs.* 15:22, 23). The man who follows his own will independently of God's is guilty of a kind of idolatry. Instead of adoring God's will, he, in a certain sense, adores his own.

The greatest glory we can give to God is to do his will in everything. Our Redeemer came on earth to glorify his heavenly Father and to teach us by his example how to do the same. St. Paul represents him saying to his eternal Father: "Sacrifice and oblation thou wouldst not: But a body thou hast fitted to me . . . Then said I: Behold I come . . . that I should do thy will, O God" (*Heb.* 10:5, 7). Thou hast refused the victims offered thee by man; thou dost will that I sacrifice my body to thee. Behold me ready to do thy will.

Our Lord frequently declared that he had come on earth not to do his own will, but solely that of his Father: "I came down from heaven, not to do my own will, but the will of him that sent me" (*John* 6:38). He spoke in the same strain in the garden when he went forth to meet his enemies who had come to seize him and to lead him to death: "But that the world may know that I love the Father: and as the Father hath given me commandment, so do I: arise and let us go hence" (*John* 14:31). Furthermore, he said he would recognize as his brother him who would do his will: "Whosoever shall do the will of my Father who is in heaven, he is my brother" (*Matt.* 12:50).

To do God's will—this was the goal upon which the saints constantly fixed their gaze. They were fully persuaded that in this consists the entire perfection of the soul. Blessed Henry Suso used to say: "It is not God's will that we should abound in spiritual delights, but that in all things we should submit to his holy will."[2] "Those who

5

give themselves to prayer," says St. Teresa, "should concentrate solely on this: the conformity of their wills with the divine will. They should be convinced that this constitutes their highest perfection. The more fully they practice this, the greater the gifts they will receive from God, and the greater the progress they will make in the interior life."[3] A certain Dominican nun was vouchsafed a vision of Heaven one day. She recognized there some persons she had known during their mortal life on earth. It was told her these souls were raised to the sublime heights of the seraphs on account of the uniformity of their wills with that of God's during their lifetime here on earth. Blessed Henry Suso, mentioned above, said of himself: "I would rather be the vilest worm on earth by God's will, than be a seraph by my own."[4]

During our sojourn in this world, we should learn from the saints now in Heaven how to love God. The pure and perfect love of God they enjoy there consists in uniting themselves perfectly to his will. It would be the greatest delight of the seraphs to pile up sand on the seashore or to pull weeds in a garden for all eternity if they found out such was God's will. Our Lord himself teaches us to ask to do the will of God on earth as the saints do it in Heaven: "Thy will be done on earth as it is in heaven" (*Matt.* 6:10).

Because David fulfilled all his wishes, God called him a man after his own heart: "I have found David . . . a man according to my own heart, who shall do all my wills" (*Acts* 13:22). David was always ready to embrace the divine will, as he frequently protested: "My heart is ready, O God, my heart is ready" (*Ps.* 56:8). He asked God for one thing alone—to teach him to do his will: "Teach me to do thy will" (*Ps.* 142:10).

A single act of uniformity with the divine will suffices to make a saint. Behold while Saul was persecuting the

Church, God enlightened him and converted him. What does Saul do? What does he say? Nothing else but to offer himself to do God's will: "Lord, what wilt thou have me to do?" (*Acts* 9:6). In return the Lord calls him a vessel of election and an apostle of the gentiles: "This man is to me a vessel of election, to carry my name before the gentiles" (*Acts* 9:15). Absolutely true—because he who gives his will to God gives him everything. He who gives his goods in alms, his blood in scourgings, his food in fasting, gives God what he has. But he who gives God his will, gives himself, gives everything he is. Such a one can say: "Though I am poor, Lord, I give thee all I possess; but when I say I give thee my will, I have nothing left to give thee." This is just what God does require of us: "My son, give me thy heart" (*Prov.* 23:26). St. Augustine's comment is: "There is nothing more pleasing we can offer God than to say to him: 'Possess thyself of us.'"[5] We cannot offer God anything more pleasing than to say: Take us, Lord, we give thee our entire will. Only let us know thy will and we will carry it out.

If we would completely rejoice the heart of God, let us strive in all things to conform ourselves to his divine will. Let us not only strive to conform ourselves, but also to unite ourselves to whatever dispositions God makes of us. *Conformity* signifies that we join our wills to the will of God. *Uniformity* means more—it means that we make one will of God's will and ours, so that we will only what God wills; that God's will alone, is our will. This is the summit of perfection and to it we should always aspire; this should be the goal of all our works, desires, meditations and prayers. To this end we should always invoke the aid of our holy patrons, our guardian angels, and above all, of our mother Mary, the most perfect of all the saints because she most perfectly embraced the divine will.

2.
Uniformity in All Things

The essence of perfection is to embrace the will of God in all things, prosperous or adverse. In prosperity, even sinners find it easy to unite themselves to the divine will; but it takes saints to unite themselves to God's will when things go wrong and are painful to self-love. Our conduct in such instances is the measure of our love of God. St. John of Avila used to say: "One 'Blessed be God' in times of adversity, is worth more than a thousand acts of gratitude in times of prosperity."[6]

Furthermore, we must unite ourselves to God's will not only in things that come to us directly from his hands, such as sickness, desolation, poverty, death of relatives, but likewise in those we suffer from man—for example, contempt, injustice, loss of reputation, loss of temporal goods and all kinds of persecution. On these occasions we must remember that while God does not will the sin, he does will our humiliation, our poverty, or our mortification, as the case may be. It is certain and of faith that whatever happens, happens by the will of God: "I form the light, and create darkness, I make peace, and create evil" (*Is.* 45:6, 7). From God come all things, good as well as evil. We call adversities evil; actually they are good and meritorious, when we receive them as coming from God's hands: "Shall there be evil in a city which the Lord hath not done?" (*Amos* 3:6). "Good things and evil, life and death, poverty and riches are from God" (*Ecclus.* 11:14).

It is true, when one offends us unjustly, God does not will his sin, nor does he concur in the sinner's bad will; but God does, in a general way, concur in the material action by which such a one strikes us, robs us or does us an injury, so that God certainly wills the offense we suffer

8

and it comes to us from his hands. Thus the Lord told David he would be the author of those things he would suffer at the hands of Absalom: "I will raise up evil against thee out of thy own house, and I will take thy wives before thy eyes and give them to thy neighbor" (*2 Kgs.* 12:11). Hence too God told the Jews that in punishment for their sins, he would send the Assyrians to plunder them and spread destruction among them: "The Assyrian . . . is the rod and staff of my anger . . . I will send him . . . to take away the spoils" (*Is.* 10:5, 6). "Assyrian wickedness served as God's scourge for the Hebrews"[7] is St. Augustine's comment on this text. And our Lord himself told St. Peter that his sacred passion came not so much from man as from his Father: "The chalice which my Father hath given me, shall I not drink it?" (*John* 18:11).

When the messenger came to announce to Job that the Sabeans had plundered his goods and slain his children, he said: "The Lord gave and the Lord hath taken away" (*Job* 1:21). He did not say: "The Lord hath given me my children and my possessions, and the Sabeans have taken them away." He realized that adversity had come upon him by the will of God. Therefore he added: "As it hath pleased the Lord, so is it done: blessed be the name of the Lord" (*Job* 1:21). We must not therefore consider the afflictions that come upon us as happening by chance or solely from the malice of men; we should be convinced that what happens, happens by the will of God. Apropos of this it is related that two martyrs, Epictetus and Atho, being put to the torture by having their bodies raked with iron hooks and burnt with flaming torches, kept repeating: "Work thy will upon us, O Lord." Arrived at the place of execution, they exclaimed: "Eternal God, be thou blessed in that thy will has been entirely accomplished in us."[8]

Cesarius points up what we have been saying by offering this incident in the life of a certain monk: Externally his religious observance was the same as that of the other monks, but he had attained such sanctity that the mere touch of his garments healed the sick. Marveling at these deeds, since his life was no more exemplary than the lives of the other monks, the superior asked him one day what was the cause of these miracles.

He replied that he too was mystified and was at a loss how to account for such happenings. "What devotions do you practice?" asked the abbot. He answered that there was little or nothing special that he did beyond making a great deal of willing only what God willed, and that God had given him the grace of abandoning his will totally to the will of God.

"Prosperity does not lift me up, nor adversity cast me down," added the monk. "I direct all my prayers to the end that God's will may be done fully in me and by me."

"That raid that our enemies made against the monastery the other day, in which our stores were plundered, our granaries put to the torch and our cattle driven off—did not this misfortune cause you any resentment?" queried the abbot.

"No, Father," came the reply. "On the contrary, I returned thanks to God—as is my custom in such circumstances—fully persuaded that God does all things, or permits all that happens, for his glory and for our greater good; thus I am always at peace, no matter what happens." Seeing such uniformity with the will of God, the abbot no longer wondered why the monk worked so many miracles.[9]

3.
Happiness Deriving from Perfect Uniformity

Acting according to this pattern, one not only becomes holy but also enjoys perpetual serenity in this life.

Alphonsus the Great, King of Aragon, being asked one day whom he considered the happiest person in the world, answered: "He who abandons himself to the will of God and accepts all things, prosperous and adverse, as coming from his hands."[10] "To them that love God, all things work together unto good" (*Rom.* 8:28). Those who love God are always happy, because their whole happiness is to fulfill, even in adversity, the will of God. Afflictions do not mar their serenity, because by accepting misfortune, they know they give pleasure to their beloved Lord: "Whatever shall befall the just man, it shall not make him sad" (*Prov.* 12:21). Indeed, what can be more satisfactory to a person than to experience the fulfillment of all his desires? This is the happy lot of the man who wills only what God wills, because everything that happens, save sin, happens through the will of God.

There is a story to this effect in the *Lives of the Fathers* about a farmer whose crops were more plentiful than those of his neighbors. On being asked how this happened with such unvarying regularity, he said he was not surprised because he always had the kind of weather he wanted. He was asked to explain. He said: "It is so because I want whatever kind of weather God wants, and because I do, he gives me the harvests I want." If souls resigned to God's will are humiliated, says Salvian,[11] they want to be humiliated; if they are poor, they want to be poor; in short, whatever happens is acceptable to them, hence they are truly at peace in this life. In cold and heat, in rain and wind, the soul united to God says: "I want it to be warm, to be cold, windy, to rain, because God wills it."

This is the beautiful freedom of the sons of God, and it is worth vastly more than all the rank and distinction of blood and birth, more than all the kingdoms in the world. This is the abiding peace which, in the experience of the saints, "surpasseth all understanding" (*Phil.* 4:7). It surpasses all pleasures rising from gratification of the senses, from social gatherings, banquets and other worldly amusements; vain and deceiving as they are, they captivate the senses for the time being, but bring no lasting contentment; rather they afflict man in the depth of his soul where alone true peace can reside.

Solomon, who tasted to satiety all the pleasures of the world and found them bitter, voiced his disillusionment thus: "But this also is vanity and vexation of spirit" (*Eccles.* 4:16). "A holy man continueth in wisdom as the sun, but a fool," says the Holy Spirit, "is changed as the moon" (*Ecclus.* 27:12). The fool, that is, the sinner, is as changeable as the moon, which today waxes and tomorrow wanes; today he laughs, tomorrow he cries; today he is meek as a lamb, tomorrow cross as a bear. Why? Because his peace of mind depends on the prosperity or the adversity he meets; he changes with the changes in the things that happen to him. The just man is like the sun, constant in his serenity, no matter what betides him. His calmness of soul is founded on his union with the will of God; hence he enjoys unruffled peace. This is the peace promised by the angel of the Nativity: "And on earth, peace to men of good will" (*Luke* 2:14). Who are these "men of good will" if not those whose wills are united to the infinitely good and perfect will of God? "The good, and the acceptable, and the perfect will of God" (*Rom.* 12:2).

By uniting themselves to the divine will, the saints have enjoyed paradise by anticipation in this life. Accustoming themselves to receive all things from the hands of God, says St. Dorotheus, the men of old maintained continual serenity of soul.[12] St. Mary Magdalene of Pazzi derived such consolation at hearing the words "will of God," that she usually fell into an ecstasy of love.[13] The instances of jangling irritation that are bound to arise will not fail to make surface impact on the senses. This however will be experienced only in the inferior part of the soul; in the superior part will reign peace and tranquillity as long as our will remains united with God's. Our Lord assured his apostles: "Your joy no man shall take from you . . . That your joy may be full" (*John* 16:22, 24). He who unites his will to God's experiences a full and lasting joy: full, because he has what he wants, as was explained above; lasting, because no one can take his joy from him, since no one can prevent what God wills from happening.

The devout Father John Tauler relates this personal experience: For years he had prayed God to send him someone who would teach him the real spiritual life. One day, at prayer, he heard a voice saying: "Go to such and such a church and you will have the answer to your prayers." He went and at the door of the church he found a beggar, barefooted and in rags. He greeted the mendicant saying: "Good day, my friend."

"Thank you, sir, for your kind wishes, but I do not recall ever having had a 'bad' day."

"Then God has certainly given you a very happy life."

"That is very true, sir. I have never been unhappy. In saying this I am not making any rash statement either. This is the reason: When I have nothing to eat, I give thanks to God; when it rains or snows, I bless God's providence; when someone insults me, drives me away, or otherwise mistreats me, I give glory to God. I said I've never had an unhappy day, and it's the truth, because I am accustomed to will unreservedly what God wills. Whatever happens to me, sweet or bitter, I gladly receive from his hands as what is best for me. Hence my unvarying happiness."

"Where did you find God?"

"I found him where I left creatures."

13

"Who are you anyway?"

"I am a king."

"And where is your kingdom?"

"In my soul, where everything is in good order; where the passions obey reason, and reason obeys God."

"How have you come to such a state of perfection?"

"By silence. I practice silence towards men, while I cultivate the habit of speaking with God. Conversing with God is the way I found and maintain my peace of soul."[14]

Union with God brought this poor beggar to the very heights of perfection. In his poverty he was richer than the mightiest monarch; in his sufferings, he was vastly happier than worldlings amid their worldly delights.

4.
God Wills Our Good

O the supreme folly of those who resist the divine will! In God's providence, no one can escape hardship: "Who resisteth his will?" (*Rom.* 9:19). A person who rails at God in adversity suffers without merit; moreover by his lack of resignation he adds to his punishment in the next life and experiences greater disquietude of mind in this life: "Who hath resisted him and hath had peace?" (*Job* 9:4). The screaming rage of the sick man in his pain, the whining complaints of the poor man in his destitution—what will they avail these people, except increase their unhappiness and bring them no relief? "Little man," says St. Augustine, "grow up. What are you seeking in your search for happiness? Seek the one good that embraces all others."[15] Whom do you seek, friend, if you seek not God? Seek him, find him, cleave to him; bind your will to his with bands of steel and you will live always at peace in this life and in the next.

God wills only our good; God loves us more than anybody else can or does love us. His will is that no one should lose his soul, that everyone should save and sanctify his soul: "Not willing that any should perish, but that all should return to penance" (*2 Ptr.* 3:9). "This is the will of God, your sanctification" (*1 Thess.* 4:3). God has made the attainment of our happiness his glory. Since he is by his nature infinite goodness, and since as St. Leo says goodness is diffusive of itself,[16] God has a supreme desire to make us sharers of his goods and of his happiness. If then he sends us suffering in this life, it is for our own good: "All things work together unto good" (*Rom.* 8:28). Even chastisements come to us, not to crush us, but to make us mend our ways and save our souls: "Let us believe that these scourges of the Lord have happened for our amendment and not for our destruction" (*Judith* 8:27).

God surrounds us with his loving care lest we suffer eternal damnation: "O Lord, thou hast crowned us as with a shield of thy good will" (*Ps.* 5:13). He is most solicitous for our welfare: "The Lord is careful for me" (*Ps.* 39:18). What can God deny us when he has given us his own son? "He that spared not even his own son, but delivered him up for us all, how hath he not also, with him, given us all things?" (*Rom.* 8:32). Therefore we should most confidently abandon ourselves to all the dispositions of divine providence, since they are for our own good. In all that happens to us, let us say: "In peace, in the selfsame I will sleep, and I will rest: For thou, O Lord, singularly hast settled me in hope" (*Ps.* 4:9, 10).

Let us place ourselves unreservedly in his hands because he will not fail to have care of us: "Casting all your care upon him, for he hath care of you" (*1 Ptr.* 5:7). Let us keep God in our thoughts and carry out his will, and he will think of us and of our welfare. Our Lord said to St. Catherine of Siena, "Daughter, think of me, and I will always think of you." Let us often repeat with the

15

Spouse in the Canticle: "My beloved to me, and I to him" (*Cant.* 2:16).

St. Niles, abbot, used to say that our petitions should be not that our wishes be done, but that God's holy will should be fulfilled in us and by us. When, therefore, something adverse happens to us, let us accept it from his hands, not only patiently, but even with gladness, as did the apostles who "went from the presence of the council rejoicing, that they were accounted worthy to suffer reproach for the name of Jesus" (*Acts* 5:41). What greater consolation can come to a soul than to know that by patiently bearing some tribulation, it gives God the greatest pleasure in its power? Spiritual writers tell us that though the desire of certain souls to please God by their sufferings is acceptable to him, still more pleasing to him is the union of certain others with his will, so that their will is neither to rejoice nor to suffer, but to hold themselves completely amenable to his will, and they desire only that his holy will be fulfilled.

If, devout soul, it is your will to please God and live a life of serenity in this world, unite yourself always and in all things to the divine will. Reflect that all the sins of your past wicked life happened because you wandered from the path of God's will. For the future, embrace God's good pleasure and say to him in every happening: "Yea, Father, for so it hath seemed good in thy sight" (*Luke* 10:21). When anything disagreeable happens, remember it comes from God and say at once, "This comes from God" and be at peace: "I was dumb and opened not my mouth, because thou hast done it" (*Ps.* 38:10). Lord, since thou hast done this, I will be silent and accept it. Direct all your thoughts and prayers to this end, to beg God constantly in meditation, Communion, and visits to the Blessed Sacrament that he help you accomplish his holy will. Form the habit of offering yourself frequently to God by saying, "My God, behold me in thy presence; do with me and all that I have as thou pleasest." This was the constant practice of St. Teresa. At least fifty times a day she offered herself to God, placing herself at his entire disposition and good pleasure.

How fortunate you, kind reader, if you too act thus! You will surely become a saint. Your life will be calm and peaceful; your death will be happy. At death all our hope of salvation will come from the testimony of our conscience as to whether or not we are dying resigned to God's will. If during life we have embraced everything as coming from God's hands, and if at death we embrace death in fulfillment of God's holy will, we shall certainly save our souls and die the death of saints. Let us then abandon everything to God's good pleasure, because being infinitely wise, he *knows* what is best for us; and being *all-good* and *all-loving*—having given his life for us—he wills what is best for us. Let us, as St. Basil counsels us, rest secure in the conviction that beyond the possibility of a doubt, God works to effect our welfare, infinitely better than we could ever hope to accomplish or desire it ourselves.

5.
Special Practices of Uniformity

Let us now take up in a practical way the consideration of those matters in which we should unite ourselves to God's will.

1. *In external matters.* In times of great heat, cold or rain; in times of famine, epidemics and similar occasions we should refrain from expressions like these: "What unbearable heat!" "What piercing cold!" "What a tragedy!" In these instances we should avoid expressions indicating opposition to God's will. We should want

things to be just as they are, because it is God who thus disposes them. An incident in point would be this one: Late one night St. Francis Borgia arrived unexpectedly at a Jesuit house, in a snowstorm. He knocked and knocked on the door, but all to no purpose because, the community being asleep, no one heard him. When morning came all were embarrassed for the discomfort he had experienced by having had to spend the night in the open. The saint, however, said he had enjoyed the greatest consolation during those long hours of the night by imagining that he saw our Lord up in the sky dropping the snowflakes down upon him.

2. *In personal matters.* In matters that affect us personally, let us acquiesce in God's will. For example, in hunger, thirst, poverty, desolation, loss of reputation, let us always say: "Do thou build up or tear down, O Lord, as seems good in thy sight. I am content. I wish only what thou dost wish." Thus too, says Rodriguez, should we act when the devil proposes certain hypothetical cases to us in order to wrest a sinful consent from us, or at least to cause us to be interiorly disturbed. For example: "What would you say or what would you do if someone were to say or do such and such a thing to you?" Let us dismiss the temptation by saying: "By God's grace, I would say or do what God would want me to say or do." Thus we shall free ourselves from imperfection and harassment.

3. Let us not lament if we suffer from some *natural defect* of body or mind; from poor memory, slowness of understanding, little ability, lameness or general bad health. What claim have we, or what obligation is God under, to give us a more brilliant mind or a more robust body? Who is ever offered a gift and then lays down the conditions upon which he will accept it? Let us thank God for what, in his pure goodness, he has given us and let us be content too with the manner in which he has

given it to us.

Who knows? Perhaps if God had given us greater talent, better health, a more personable appearance, we might have lost our souls! Great talent and knowledge have caused many to be puffed up with the idea of their own importance and, in their pride, they have despised others. How easily those who have these gifts fall into grave danger to their salvation! How many on account of physical beauty or robust health have plunged headlong into a life of debauchery! How many, on the contrary, who, by reason of poverty, infirmity or physical deformity, have become saints and have saved their souls, who, given health, wealth or physical attractiveness had else lost their souls! Let us then be content with what God has given us. "But one thing is necessary" (*Luke* 10:42), and it is not beauty, not health, not talent. It is the salvation of our immortal souls.

4. It is especially necessary that we be resigned in *corporal infirmities*. We should willingly embrace them in the manner and for the length of time that God wills. We ought to make use of the ordinary remedies in time of sickness—such is God's will; but if they are not effective, let us unite ourselves to God's will and this will be better for us than would be our restoration to health. Let us say: "Lord, I wish neither to be well nor to remain sick; I want only what thou wilt." Certainly, it is more virtuous not to repine in times of painful illness; still and all, when our sufferings are excessive, it is not wrong to let our friends know what we are enduring, and also to ask God to free us from our sufferings. Let it be understood, however, that the sufferings here referred to are actually excessive. It often happens that some, on the occasion of a slight illness, or even a slight indisposition, want the whole world to stand still and sympathize with them in their illnesses.

But where it is a case of real suffering, we have the example of our Lord, who, at the approach of his bitter passion, made known his state of soul to his disciples, saying: "My soul is sorrowful even unto death" (*Matt.* 26:38), and besought his eternal Father to deliver him from it: "Father, if it be possible, let this chalice pass from me" (*Matt.* 26:39). But our Lord likewise taught us what we should do when we have made such a petition when he added: "Nevertheless, not as I will, but as thou wilt" (*Matt.* 26:39).

How childish the pretense of those who protest they wish for health not to escape suffering, but to serve our Lord better by being able to observe their Rule, to serve the community, go to church, receive Communion, do penance, study, work for souls in the confessional and pulpit! Devout soul, tell me, why do you desire to do these things? To please God? Why then search any further to please God when you are sure God does not wish these prayers, Communions, penances or studies, but he does wish that you suffer patiently this sickness he sends you? Unite then your sufferings to those of our Lord.

"But," you say, "I do not want to be sick for then I am useless, a burden to my Order, to my monastery." But if you are united to and resigned to God's will, you will realize that your superiors are likewise resigned to the dispositions of divine providence, and that they recognize the fact that you are a burden, not through indolence, but by the will of God. Ah, how often these desires and these laments are born, not of the love of God, but of the love of self! How many of them are so many pretexts for fleeing the will of God! Do we want to please God? When we find ourselves confined to our sickbed, let us utter this one prayer: "Thy will be done." Let us repeat it time and time again and it will please God more than all our mortifications and devotions. There is no better way to serve

God than cheerfully to embrace his holy will.

St. John of Avila once wrote to a sick priest: "My dear friend—Do not weary yourself planning what you would do if you were well, but be content to be sick for as long as God wishes. If you are seeking to carry out God's will, what difference should it make to you whether you are sick or well?"[17] The saint was perfectly right, for God is glorified not by our works, but by our resignation to, and by our union with, his holy will. In this respect St. Francis de Sales used to say we serve God better by our sufferings than by our actions.

Many times it will happen that proper medical attention or effective remedies will be lacking, or even that the doctor will not rightly diagnose our case. In such instances we must unite ourselves to the divine will which thus disposes of our physical health. The story is told of a client of St. Thomas of Canterbury, who being sick, went to the saint's tomb to obtain a cure. He returned home cured. But then he thought to himself: "Suppose it would be better for my soul's salvation if I remained sick, what point then is there in being well?" In this frame of mind he went back and asked the saint to intercede with God that he grant what would be best for his eternal salvation. His illness returned and he was perfectly content with the turn things had taken, being fully persuaded that God had thus disposed of him for his own good.

There is a similar account by Surio to the effect that a certain blind man obtained the restoration of his sight by praying to St. Bedasto, bishop. Thinking the matter over, he prayed again to his heavenly patron, but this time with the purpose that if the possession of his sight were not expedient for his soul, that his blindness should return. And that is exactly what happened—he was blind again. Therefore, in sickness it is better that we seek neither sickness nor health, but that we abandon ourselves

21

to the will of God so that he may dispose of us as he wishes. However, if we decide to ask for health, let us do so at least always resigned and with the proviso that our bodily health may be conducive to the health of our soul. Otherwise our prayer will be defective and will remain unheard because our Lord does not answer prayers made without resignation to his holy will.

Sickness is the acid test of spirituality because it discloses whether our virtue is real or sham. If the soul is not agitated, does not break out in lamentations, is not feverishly restless in seeking a cure, but instead is submissive to the doctors and to superiors, is serene and tranquil, completely resigned to God's will, it is a sign that that soul is well-grounded in virtue.

What of the whiner who complains of lack of attention? That his sufferings are beyond endurance? That the doctor does not know his business? What of the faint-hearted soul who laments that the hand of God is too heavy upon him?

This story by St. Bonaventure in his *Life of St. Francis* is in point: On a certain occasion when the saint was suffering extraordinary physical pain, one of his religious, meaning to sympathize with him, said in his simplicity: "My Father, pray God that he treat you a little more gently, for his hand seems heavy upon you just now." Hearing this, St. Francis strongly resented the unhappy remark of his well-meaning brother, saying: "My good brother, did I not know that what you have just said was spoken in all simplicity, without realizing the implication of your words, I should never see you again because of your rashness in passing judgment on the dispositions of divine providence." Whereupon, weak and wasted as he was by his illness, he got out of bed, knelt down, kissed the floor and prayed thus: "Lord, I thank thee for the sufferings thou art sending me. Send me more, if it be thy good pleasure. My pleasure is that you afflict me and spare me not, for the fulfillment of thy holy will is the greatest consolation of my life."

6.
Spiritual Desolation

We ought to view in the light of God's holy will the loss of persons who are helpful to us in a spiritual or material way. Pious souls often fail in this respect by not being resigned to the dispositions of God's holy will. Our sanctification comes fundamentally and essentially from God, not from spiritual directors. When God sends us a spiritual director, he wishes us to use him for our spiritual profit; but if he takes him away, he wants us to remain calm and unperturbed and to increase our confidence in his goodness by saying to him: "Lord, thou hast given me this help and now thou dost take it away. Blessed be thy holy will! I beg thee, teach me what I must do to serve thee."

In this manner too we should receive whatever other crosses God sends us. "But," you reply, "these sufferings are really punishments." The answer to that remark is: Are not the punishments God sends us in this life also graces and benefits? Our offenses against God must be atoned for somehow, either in this life or in the next. Hence we should all make St. Augustine's prayer our own: "Lord, here cut, here burn and spare me not, but spare me in eternity!" Let us say with Job: "That this may be my comfort, that afflicting me with sorrow, he spare not" (*Job* 6:10). Having merited hell for our sins, we should be consoled that God chastises us in this life, and animate ourselves to look upon such treatment as a pledge that God wishes to spare us in the next. When God sends us punishments let us say with the high-priest Heli: "It is the

Lord, let him do what is good in his sight" (*1 Kgs.* 3:18).

The time of spiritual desolation is also a time for being resigned. When a soul begins to cultivate the spiritual life, God usually showers his consolations upon her to wean her away from the world; but when he sees her making solid progress, he withdraws his hand to test her and to see if she will love and serve him without the reward of sensible consolations. "In this life," as St. Teresa used to say, "our lot is not to enjoy God, but to do his holy will." And again, "Love of God does not consist in experiencing his tendernesses, but in serving him with resolution and humility." And in yet another place, "God's true lovers are discovered in times of aridity and temptation."

Let the soul thank God when she experiences his loving endearments, but let her not repine when she finds herself left in desolation. It is important to lay great stress on this point because some souls, beginners in the spiritual life, finding themselves in spiritual aridity, think God has abandoned them, or that the spiritual life is not for them; thus they give up the practice of prayer and lose what they have previously gained. The time of aridity is the best time to practice resignation to God's holy will. I do not say you will feel no pain in seeing yourself deprived of the sensible presence of God; it is impossible for the soul not to feel it and lament over it, when even our Lord cried out on the cross: "My God, my God, why hast thou forsaken me?" (*Matt.* 27:46). In her sufferings, however, the soul should always be resigned to God's will.

The saints have all experienced desolations and abandonment of soul. "How impervious to things spiritual, my heart!" cries St. Bernard. "No savor in pious reading, no pleasure in meditation nor in prayer!" For the most part it has been the common lot of the saints to encounter aridities; sensible consolations were the exceptions. Such things are rare occurrences granted to untried souls so that they may not halt on the road to sanctity; the real delights and happiness that will constitute their reward are reserved for Heaven. This earth is a place of merit which is acquired by suffering; Heaven is a place of reward and happiness. Hence, in this life the saints neither desired nor sought the joys of sensible fervor, but rather the fervor of the spirit toughened in the crucible of suffering. "O how much better it is," says St. John of Avila, "to endure aridity and temptation by God's will than to be raised to the heights of contemplation without God's will!"

But you say you would gladly endure desolation if you were certain that it comes from God, but you are tortured by the anxiety that your desolation comes by your own fault and is a punishment for your tepidity. Very well, let us suppose you are right; then get rid of your tepidity and exercise more diligence in the affairs of your soul. But because you are possibly experiencing spiritual darkness, are you going to get all wrought up, give up prayer, and thus make things twice as bad as they are?

Let us assume that this aridity is a punishment for your tepidity. Was it not God who sent it? Accept your desolation, as your just desserts and unite yourself to God's holy will. Did you not say that you merited hell? And now you are complaining? Perhaps you think God should send you consolations! Away with such ideas and be patient under God's hand. Take up your prayers again and continue to walk in the way you have entered upon; for the future, fear lest such laments come from too little humility and too little resignation to the will of God. Therefore be resigned and say: "Lord, I accept this punishment from thy hands, and I accept it for as long as it pleases thee; if it be thy will that I should be thus afflicted for all eternity, I am satisfied." Such a prayer, though hard to make, will be far more advantageous to you than the sweetest sensible consolations.

It is well to remember, however, that aridity is not always a chastisement; at times it is a disposition of divine providence for our greater spiritual profit and to keep us humble. Lest St. Paul become vain on account of the spiritual gifts he had received, the Lord permitted him to be tempted to impurity: "And lest the greatness of the revelations should exalt me, there was given me a sting of my flesh, an angel of Satan to buffet me" (*2 Cor.* 12:7).

Prayer made amid sensible devotion is not much of an achievement: "There is a friend, a companion at the table, and he will not abide in the day of distress" (*Ecclus.* 6:10). You would not consider the casual guest at your table a friend, but only him who assists you in your need without thought of benefit to himself. When God sends spiritual darkness and desolation, his true friends are known.

Palladius, the author of the *Lives of the Fathers of the Desert,* experiencing great disgust in prayer, went seeking advice from the abbot Macarius. The saintly abbot gave him this counsel: "When you are tempted in times of dryness to give up praying because you seem to be wasting your time, say: 'Since I cannot pray, I will be satisfied just to remain on watch here in my cell for the love of Jesus Christ!'" Devout soul, you do the same when you are tempted to give up prayer just because you seem to be getting nowhere. Say: "I am going to stay here just to please God." St. Francis de Sales used to say that if we do nothing else but banish distractions and temptations in our prayers, the prayer is well made. Tauler states that persevering prayer in time of dryness will receive greater grace than prayer made amid great sensible devotion.

Rodriguez cites the case of a person who persevered forty years in prayer despite aridity, and experienced great spiritual strength as a result of it; on occasion, when through aridity he would omit meditation he felt spiritually weak and incapable of good deeds. St. Bonaventure and Gerson both say that persons who do not experience the recollection they would like to have in their meditations often serve God better than they would do if they did have it; the reason is that lack of recollection keeps them more diligent and humble; otherwise they would become puffed up with spiritual pride and grow tepid, vainly believing they had reached the summit of sanctity.

What has been said of dryness holds true of temptations also. Certainly we should strive to avoid temptations; but if God wishes that we be tempted against faith, purity, or any other virtue, we should not give in to discouraging lamentations, but submit ourselves with resignation to God's holy will. St. Paul asked to be freed from temptations to impurity and our Lord answered him, saying: "My grace is sufficient for thee" (*2 Cor.* 12:9).

So should we act when we find ourselves victims of unrelenting temptations and God seemingly deaf to our prayers. Let us then say: "Lord, do with me, let happen to me what thou wilt; thy grace is sufficient for me. Only never let me lose this grace." Consent to temptation, not temptation of itself, can make us lose the grace of God. Temptation resisted keeps us humble, brings us greater merit, makes us have frequent recourse to God, thus preserving us from offending him and uniting us more closely to him in the bonds of his holy love.

Finally, we should be united to God's will in regard to the time and manner of our death. One day St. Gertrude, while climbing up a small hill, lost her footing and fell into a ravine below. After her companions had come to her assistance, they asked her if while falling she had any fear of dying without the sacraments. "I earnestly hope and desire to have the benefit of the sacraments when death is at hand; still, to my way of thinking, the will of God is more important. I believe that the best disposition I could have to die a happy death would be to submit myself to whatever God would wish in my regard. For this reason I desire whatever kind of death God will be pleased to send me."

In his *Dialogues*, St. Gregory tells of a certain priest, Santolo by name, who was captured by the Vandals and condemned to death. The barbarians told him to choose the manner of his death. He refused, saying: "I am in God's hands and I gladly accept whatever kind of death he wishes me to suffer at your hands; I wish no other." This reply was so pleasing to God that he miraculously stayed the hand of the executioner ready to behead him. The barbarians were so impressed by the miracle that they freed their prisoner. As regards the manner of our death, therefore, we should esteem that the best kind of death for us which God has designed for us. When therefore we think of our death, let our prayer be: "O Lord, only let me save my soul and I leave the manner of my death to thee!"[18]

We should likewise unite ourselves to God's will when the moment of death is near. What else is this earth but a prison where we suffer and where we are in constant danger of losing God? Hence David prayed: "Bring my soul out of prison" (*Ps.* 141:8). St. Teresa too feared to lose God and when she would hear the striking of the clock, she would find consolation in the thought that the passing of the hour was an hour less of the danger of losing God.

St. John of Avila was convinced that every right-minded person should desire death on account of living in peril of losing divine grace. What can be more pleasant or desirable than, by dying a good death, to have the assurance of no longer being able to lose the grace of

God? Perhaps you will answer that you have as yet done nothing to deserve this reward. If it were God's will that your life should end now, what would you be doing, living on here against his will? Who knows, you might fall into sin and be lost! Even if you escaped mortal sin, you could not live free from all sin. "Why are we so tenacious of life," exclaims St. Bernard, "when the longer we live, the more we sin?"[19] A single venial sin is more displeasing to God than all the good works we can perform.

Moreover, the person who has little desire for Heaven shows he has little love for God. The true lover desires to be with his beloved. We cannot see God while we remain here on earth; hence the saints have yearned for death so that they might go and behold their beloved Lord, face to face. "Oh, that I might die and behold thy beautiful face!" sighed St. Augustine. And St. Paul: "Having a desire to be dissolved and to be with Christ" (*Phil.* 1:23). "When shall I come and appear before the face of God?" (*Ps.* 41:3) exclaimed the psalmist.

A hunter one day heard the voice of a man singing most sweetly in the forest. Following the sound, he came upon a leper horribly disfigured by the ravages of his disease. Addressing him he said: "How can you sing when you are so terribly afflicted and your death is so near at hand?" And the leper: "Friend, my poor body is a crumbling wall and it is the only thing that separates me from my God. When it falls I shall go forth to God. Time for me is indeed fast running out, so every day I show my happiness by lifting my voice in song."

Lastly, we should unite ourselves to the will of God as regards our degree of grace and glory. True, we should esteem the things that make for the glory of God, but we should show the greatest esteem for those that concern the will of God. We should desire to love God more than the seraphs, but not to a degree higher than God has des-

29

tined for us. St. John of Avila says: "I believe every saint has had the desire to be higher in grace than he actually was. However, despite this, their serenity of soul always remained unruffled. Their desire for a greater degree of grace sprang not from a consideration of their own good, but of God's. They were content with the degree of grace God had meted out for them, though actually God had given them less. They considered it a greater sign of true love of God to be content with what God had given them, than to desire to have received more."[20]

This means, as Rodriguez explains it, we should be diligent in striving to become perfect, so that tepidity and laziness may not serve as excuses for some to say: "God must help me; I can do only so much for myself." Nevertheless, when we do fall into some fault, we should not lose our peace of soul and union with the will of God, which permits our fall; nor should we lose our courage. Let us rise at once from this fall, penitently humbling ourselves and by seeking greater help from God, let us continue to march resolutely on the highway of the spiritual life. Likewise, we may well desire to be among the seraphs in Heaven, not for our own glory, but for God's, and to love him more; still we should be resigned to his will and be content with that degree of glory which in his mercy he has set for us.

It would be a serious defect to desire the gifts of supernatural prayer—specifically, ecstasies, visions and revelations. The masters of the spiritual life say that souls thus favored by God should ask him to take them away so that they may love him out of pure faith—a way of greater security. Many have come to perfection without these supernatural gifts; the only virtues worth-while are those that draw the soul to holiness of life, namely, the virtue of uniformity with God's holy will. If God does not wish to raise us to the heights of perfection and glory, let us unite ourselves in all things to his holy will, asking him in his mercy to grant us our soul's salvation. If we act in this manner, the reward will not be slight which we shall receive from the hands of God who loves above all others souls resigned to his holy will.

7.
Conclusion

Finally we should consider the events which are happening to us now and which will happen to us in the future as coming from the hands of God. Everything we do should be directed to this one end: to do the will of God and to do it solely for the reason that God wills it. To walk more securely on this road we must depend on the guidance of our superiors in external matters, and on our directors in internal matters, to learn from them God's will in our regard, having great faith in the words of our Lord: "He that heareth you, heareth me" (*Luke* 10:16).

Above all, let us bend all our energies to serve God in the way he wishes. This remark is made so that we may avoid the mistake of him who wastes his time in idle daydreaming. Such a one says, "If I were to become a hermit, I would become a saint" or "If I were to enter a monastery, I would practice penance" or "If I were to go away from here, leaving friends and companions, I would devote long hours to prayer." If, If, If—all these if's! In the meantime such a person goes from bad to worse. These idle fancies are often temptations of the devil, because they are not in accord with God's will. Hence we should dismiss them summarily and rouse ourselves to serve God only in that way which he has marked out for us. Doing his holy will, we shall certainly become holy in those surroundings in which he has placed us.

Let us will always and ever only what God wills; for so

doing, he will press us to his heart. To this end let us familiarize ourselves with certain texts of sacred scripture that invite us to unite ourselves constantly with the divine will: "Lord, what wilt thou have me do?" (*Acts* 9:6). Tell me, my God, what thou wilt have me do, that I may will it also, with all my heart. "I am thine, save thou me" (*Ps.* 118:94). I am no longer my own, I am thine, O Lord, do with me as thou wilt.

If some particularly crushing misfortune comes upon us, for example, the death of a relative, loss of goods, let us say: "Yea, Father, for so it hath seemed good in thy sight" (*Matt.* 11:26). Yes, my God and my Father, so be it, for such is thy good pleasure. Above all, let us cherish that prayer of our Lord, which he himself taught us: "Thy will be done on earth as it is in heaven" (*Matt.* 6:10). Our Lord bade St. Catherine of Genoa to make a notable pause at these words whenever she said the Our Father, praying that God's holy will be fulfilled on earth with the same perfection with which the saints do it in Heaven. Let this be our practice also, and we shall certainly become saints.

May the divine will be loved and praised! May the Immaculate Virgin be also praised!

CITATION IN PREFACE

1. Saggio Storico di Prof. Candido M. Romano, Roma Libreria Salesiano, 1896.

CITATIONS IN THE TEXT

1. St. Dionysius the Areopagite, *De divinus nominibus*, c. 4.
2. L. 2, c. 4.
3. *Obras Completas de Santa Teresa de Jesus*, 4:27, 28.
4. *Sermon 2* (Opera Colon Agrippa).
5. *Commentary on Psalm 131:3*.
6. *Spiritual Letters*, 41.
7. *Commentary on Psalm 73*.
8. *Lives of the Fathers*, 73-402, etc.
9. *Dialogue distin.*, cap. 9.
10. Antonius Panormita, *De dictis et factis Alphonsus regis*, bk. 4.
11. *De gubernatione Dei*, bk. 1, no. 2.
12. *Doctrina*, 7:4 & 6.
13. Puccine, *Vita*, part 1, chap. 59.
14. *The Inner Way: Thirty-Six Sermons for Festivals*, p. 473ff.
15. *Opera Cap.*, 34, ML 40-966.
16. *Sermon XXII on the Feast of the Nativity II*, cap. 1.
17. *Spiritual Letters*, 2.
18. Bk. 3, chap. 37.
19. *Meditations*, chap. 8.
20. *Audi Fili*, c. 13.